Claim Your

www.questionsabou[...]

MW00576594

Like our Facebook page
@QuestionsAboutMe

Follow us on Instagram
@QuestionsAboutMe_Official

Questions & Customer Service
hello@questionsaboutme.com

1000 Would You Rather Questions About Me

by Questions About Me™

www.questionsaboutme.com

Introduction

Communication is key for meaningful relationships, but we often rely on small talk and dull exchanges without truly engaging others in deep conversation.

1000 Would You Rather Questions About Me is a tool to help spark engaging discussions and thoughts. You can use *1000 Would You Rather Questions About Me* to unlock endless conversational possibilities with someone you've known for years or someone you've recently met.

Enjoy learning more about yourself and foster conversation and engagement with others.

Ask yourself these dilemma-style questions or use them as conversation prompts with family and friends—even strangers!—to cultivate meaningful and fun discussions. These thought-provoking dilemmas will help you communicate and connect in an easy and entertaining way.

We've intentionally made the questions random so they're spontaneous. The dilemmas have been created for adults, but they're suitable for children as young as nine years old—we've included some extra easy questions for younger audiences.

Our *Questions About Me* series is for everyone—there's no adult content and the questions are free from political affiliation and religious preference.

How to Use this Book

» You must choose an answer! The dilemmas will make you think and force you to make a choice.

» Going deeper with your answers by explaining your logic will lead to rewarding explorations and discussions.

» Don't be afraid to go off-topic. The wide range of intriguing scenarios will result in interesting conversations, lively discussions, and endless laughs!

» The format of this book is flexible and the questions can be tackled any way you like. You can skip around and answer questions, or you can start at the beginning and work through them in order.

» The writing space is purposely limited so you can use this book as a tool in a variety of ways—ask the questions out loud, fill in your responses, or answer the questions in your journal.

» Put down your phone, switch off the TV, and declare the time you spend answering these questions a no-judgment zone.

» Remember, there are no correct or incorrect answers. Allow yourself to be vulnerable and don't hold back with your responses.

You can enjoy our *Questions About Me* series on your own, one-on-one, or in a group setting.

Yourself

» Use as a guided journal, or question-a-day journal, for writing prompts or for creative inspiration.
» Complete the questions as a mindfulness activity for self-reflection, personal growth, and better self-understanding.
» Give a completed book to someone special as a keepsake.
» Offer it as a unique and thoughtful gift to friends, family, a significant other, or yourself.

One-on-one

» Take turns asking questions with your significant other. Strengthen your relationship and bond with your partner by learning more about each other. (You could also get your partner to answer the questions as if they were you.)
» Deepen your knowledge of those closest to you. Discover new things information about your kids, parents, siblings, and close friends with questions you never thought to ask.

Group discussions

» Stir up fun conversations at gatherings with family or friends at the dinner table, family events, or as a holiday activity.
» Download the book and use while traveling.
» Level up your conversation skills at networking events, team-building games, business trips, ice-breaker activities, job interviews, or therapy sessions.

The most important thing to know about using this book is: **There is no wrong way to use this book.** What's important is that you have fun.

No matter how you choose to use this book, enjoy using our *Questions About Me* series in any context or social situation to ignite meaningful connections and conversations.

01   WYR lose an arm or a leg?

02   WYR be too hot or too cold?

03   WYR live in a world where nothing is square or one where nothing is round?

04   WYR be caught in an earthquake or a tornado?

05   WYR give up chocolate or give up cheese?

06   WYR be the size of a giraffe or the size of an ant for the day?

07   WYR hang out with King Arthur or Robin Hood?

08   WYR have a tree house or an underground bunker?

09   WYR eat your least favorite food once a week or eat your favorite food only once a week?

10   WYR be able to swim like a fish or climb like a gecko?

11   WYR all your clothes had to be fastened with buttons or with zippers?

12   WYR reduce or recycle?

13   WYR have hiccups or a persistent cough for the day?

14   WYR be a world-class tap dancer or a world-class line dancer?

15   WYR shave off your hair or shave off your eyebrows?

16   WYR never eat red-colored food or never eat green-colored food again?

17   WYR never cut your fingernails or never cut your toenails again?

18   WYR have fur or feathers?

19   WYR visit the moon or the bottom of the deepest ocean?

20   WYR always be twenty minutes early or always be ten minutes late?

21   WYR have the go-ahead to get to the front of any line or always have traffic lights go green as you approach?

22   WYR be a boy named Sue or a girl named Hank?

23   WYR know everything there is to know or have access to the resources to research everything?

24   WYR have one lifelong friend or lots of short-term friends?

25   WYR find the key to a secret door or the key to a secret box?

26   WYR come face to face with a vampire or a werewolf?

27   WYR have an attic or a basement in your home?

28   WYR forget how to read or forget how to write?

29   WYR float like a butterfly or sting like a bee?

30   WYR have no heating or no air conditioning?

31   WYR end world poverty or find a cure for cancer?

32   WYR be fluent in three languages or be able to talk to animals?

33   WYR have hooves or claws?

34   WYR be a fly on the wall or a snake in the grass?

35   WYR have the speed of a cheetah or the strength of a gorilla?

36   WYR take a risk or play it safe?

37   WYR have no hot water in your home or no indoor toilet?

38   WYR love your job and get paid a little or hate your job and get paid a lot?

39   WYR be attacked by two angry geese or six angry Chihuahuas?

40   WYR be able to make your own clothes or grow your own food?

41   WYR have to sing everything you say or repeat everything you say?

42   WYR be able to breathe underwater or see in the dark?

43   WYR be invisible or be able to read minds?

44   WYR be the best musician in a little-known band or the weakest musician in a well-known band?

45 WYR win the Nobel Prize for Medicine or for Peace?

46 WYR have permanent dandruff or a constantly runny nose?

47 WYR be as sly as a fox or as gentle as a lamb?

48 WYR a professional photographer took your picture or a professional stylist styled your hair?

49 WYR never have to work again or never have to pay bills again?

50 WYR have the eye of the tiger or eyes like a hawk?

51 WYR accidentally brush your teeth with soap or wash your hair with toilet cleaner?

52 WYR your eyes could see like a microscope or far into the distance like binoculars?

53 WYR lose the money you made this year or the memories you made this year?

54 WYR have ninja-like stealth or gladiator-like strength?

55 WYR eat dinner alone for a year or eat with a group of people you don't like for a year?

56 WYR be able to press a fast-forward button or a rewind button in your life?

57 WYR be the first or the last to know the world is ending?

58 WYR your face aged ten years overnight or your body from the neck down aged fifteen years overnight?

59 WYR have someone constantly finish your sentences or someone constantly interrupt your conversations?

60 WYR an alarm sounded every time you said a curse word or every time you lied?

61 WYR be able to run but have nowhere to hide or hide and have nowhere to run?

62 WYR have your toes stepped on every day or your hair pulled every day?

63 WYR be able to play every musical instrument or sing every song?

64 WYR wear shoes that turned you into an excellent dancer or shoes that gave you super running speed?

65 WYR collect something few people care about or be an expert in something few people want to know?

66 WYR be accused of something you didn't do or have someone else take the credit for something you did do?

67 WYR be stuck in an elevator with a bragger or a moaner?

68 WYR be able to do only one magical spell well or do lots of spells with only a fifty percent chance of success?

69 WYR be known for being kind or for being someone no one should mess with?

70 WYR have been born a decade earlier or a decade later than you were?

71 WYR be able to walk through walls or see through walls?

72 WYR have the cleanliness of your fridge or your oven inspected right now?

73 WYR everyone laughed when you walk into a room or everyone cried?

74 WYR tell the truth, no matter what, or tell a lie to save a friend?

75 WYR make snap decisions using your heart or your head?

76 WYR be the bearer of bad news or receive bad news?

77 WYR be locked in a room with no source of light or locked in room with a bright light permanently on?

78 WYR be once bitten, twice shy or be in for a penny, in for a pound?

79 WYR be able to clear traffic jams by clapping your hands or get instant takeout by snapping your fingers?

80 WYR be trapped in a romantic comedy with your enemies or trapped in a horror movie with your friends?

81 WYR fail your driving test six times or get dumped six times in a row?

82 WYR be homeless or live alone with no family and friends?

83 WYR die of starvation or sell one of your kidneys to buy food?

84 WYR be reincarnated as a beautiful butterfly with a short life or a stray dog living on the street?

85 WYR be a notorious baddie everyone loves to hate or an unsung hero?

86 WYR eat only your favorite meal for every meal or never eat your favorite meal again?

87 WYR be an early riser or a night owl?

88 WYR be known as witty or wise?

89 WYR live in a world where you never had to work again or one where you never had to sleep again?

90 WYR wear dirty clothes or torn clothes?

91 WYR be in a dull, long-lasting relationship or an exciting, short-lived relationship?

92 WYR never eat out or eat out once a week at a five-star restaurant for free with someone you don't like?

93 WYR be like someone else or stay as you are?

94 WYR end all war or find a cure for all disease?

95   WYR work your way from rags to riches or win the lottery?

96   WYR noisy neighbors kept you awake or nosy neighbors watched your every move?

97   WYR have shorter work hours each week or longer vacations each year?

98   WYR work in a team or work alone?

99   WYR hear the bad news or the good news first?

100 WYR be your own boss or work for an awesome boss?

101 WYR invent an instant weight-loss plan that works or an anti-aging cream that works?

102 WYR stand out from the crowd or blend into the background?

103 WYR cut your hand off to escape death or abandon a friend in danger to escape death?

104 WYR have a toothache or an earache for a week?

105 WYR have too little time and so much to do or have too little to do and so much time?

106 WYR be the first person to step onto the rickety rope bridge or the last person in line for the lifeboat?

107 WYR be in an arranged marriage or remain single for life?

108 WYR babysit a crying baby or have a noisy teenage houseguest?

109 WYR go speed dating or have a friend set you up on a blind date?

110 WYR wear the same underpants or the same socks for two days?

111 WYR slide down the banister or swing from the chandelier?

112 WYR learn how to eat fire or learn how to ride a motorcycle wall of death?

113 WYR ride a unicorn or swim with a mermaid?

114 WYR tiptoe through the tulips or walk on the wild side?

115 WYR be able to see through walls or listen in on conversations a block away?

116   WYR spend three weeks in prison or six weeks under house arrest?

117   WYR be indestructible or invisible?

118   WYR have your face on the front cover of a magazine or your name on the front of a book?

119   WYR prove the existence of the Loch Ness Monster or leprechauns?

120   WYR be hugely famous for a few years in your lifetime or achieve fame after your death?

121   WYR be green with envy or red with anger?

122   WYR smell the aroma of freshly baked bread or freshly cut flowers?

123   WYR be able to talk to trees or interpret whale song?

124   WYR only be able to eat raw foods or only be able to eat canned foods?

125   WYR be able to move things with your mind or read other people's minds?

126 WYR have no sense of humor or have no one ever laugh at your jokes?

127 WYR never cry again or never dance again?

128 WYR have a film crew follow your every move for a week or have zero contact with anyone for a week?

129 WYR never be able to run again or never be able to sing again?

130 WYR die surrounded by family at the age of 40 or outlive most of your family and die at the age of 104?

131 WYR live in your dream house in your least favorite location or an ugly house in your favorite location?

132 WYR see no daylight for a month or be under nighttime curfew for a month?

133 WYR go from riches to rags or from A-lister to nobody?

134 WYR discover a dark family secret or have a skeleton in your closet revealed?

135 WYR buy no new clothes for a year or have new clothes every day chosen for you by someone else?

136   WYR be the butt of a joke or be the last person to get the joke?

137   WYR not know where your next meal is coming from or not know where you're sleeping tonight?

138   WYR only get to change your clothes once a week or have a shower once a week?

139   WYR be hungry or be tired?

140   WYR have an amazing body and a plain face or a gorgeous face and a not-so-great body?

141   WYR someone rained on your parade or be told you are a wet blanket?

142   WYR look twenty-one years old physically or feel twenty-one years old mentally?

143   WYR be a one-hit wonder as a best-selling author or as the singer of a chart-topping novelty song?

144   WYR be a contestant on a TV game show or a reality TV survival show?

145   WYR be in the history books as a renowned scientist or a renowned artist?

146   WYR have blacksmithing skills or surgical skills?

147   WYR have too many friends or too few?

148   WYR sing in front of friends or in front of strangers?

149   WYR have retractable claws or razor-sharp teeth?

150   WYR accidentally shoot yourself in the foot or chop off a finger?

151   WYR be very talented or extremely lucky?

152   WYR live with messy but fun housemates or tidy but boring housemates?

153   WYR live without electricity for two days or live without hot food for a week?

154   WYR have cosmetic surgery to change your nose or change your teeth?

155   WYR literally have eyes in the back of your head or literally have lightning reflexes?

156   WYR never get married or never have a best friend?

157   WYR rescue the three-legged puppy or the one-eyed kitten from the animal shelter?

158   WYR have been a pioneer on a wagon train or a team member of the Apollo 11 moon mission?

159   WYR be the brightest star in the sky or the tallest mountain in the range?

160   WYR find proof of alien life or find proof there's no other life in the universe?

161   WYR be quarantined for three months alone or with extended family members?

162   WYR wake up to find your hair had fallen out or your teeth had fallen out?

163   WYR be typecast as a rom-com sweetie or an evil villain?

164   WYR have super-strength by night or a photographic memory by day?

165   WYR be a Formula One driver or a Red Bull Air Race pilot?

166   WYR have a frantic Friday or a manic Monday?

167   WYR be in prison for a year or homeless for a year?

168   WYR have sweaty palms or sweaty armpits on a first date?

169   WYR never dance again or dance nonstop for forty-eight hours?

170   WYR be able to ride a unicycle or spin plates?

171   WYR never be in debt or never eat ice cream again?

172   WYR have an excellent poker face or wear your heart on your sleeve?

173   WYR find a dragon's treasure or a pirate's treasure?

174   WYR live in a world with giant earthworms or giant birds?

175   WYR be stuck in an elevator with two grumpy people or one sweet person with two smelly dogs?

176   WYR snort like a pig when you laugh or bray like a donkey when you laugh?

177   WYR be able to bring the pictures you draw to life or be able to step into the pictures in storybooks?

178   WYR be deaf in one ear or blind in one eye?

179   WYR wear a mohawk hairstyle for a month or clown makeup every
day for a month?

180   WYR control gravity or control time?

181   WYR be hopelessly underdressed or more than fashionably late for
important events?

182   WYR be all-powerful or all-knowing?

183   WYR be able to switch your sense of smell on and off or switch
your emotions on and off?

184   WYR have an ugly phone with awesome features or an awesome-
looking phone with only standard features?

185   WYR have your last phone conversation broadcast on national
radio or your last thought appear in words over your head?

186   WYR end animal testing or ban zoos?

187   WYR invent a solution to world pollution or world hunger?

188 WYR go to work in your party clothes or go to a party in your work clothes?

189 WYR save a stranger's life by giving CPR or help a stranger give birth?

190 WYR get dressed in the dark or wear your clothes back to front?

191 WYR avoid black cats crossing your path or walking under ladders?

192 WYR poke yourself in the eye or bite your tongue?

193 WYR be a beekeeper or bookkeeper?

194 WYR jump rope or bounce on a trampoline?

195 WYR feed the birds or water the plants?

196 WYR spend a rainy afternoon in a library or in a museum?

197 WYR sing-along so hard your voice cracks or laugh so hard your sides hurt?

198 WYR have an easy job working for someone else or work for yourself but work really hard?

199   WYR go out without brushing your hair or without brushing your teeth?

200   WYR comfort-eat with a whole carton of ice cream or a whole bucket of chicken wings?

201   WYR have an annoying song stuck in your head or the feeling you're about to sneeze for an hour?

202   WYR have a personal trainer or a personal chauffeur?

203   WYR learn an alien language or teach your language to an alien?

204   WYR buy more than you need at the grocery store or forget the one thing you need?

205   WYR lose your short-term memory or your long-term memory?

206   WYR be able to predict your own future or the future of the world?

207   WYR live with a ghost in your house or be a ghost in someone else's house?

208   WYR be ignored or have everything you say and do criticized?

209   WYR clean up after every party you attend or never go to another party?

210   WYR have no power or no water in your home for a week?

211   WYR be a horse whisperer or a lion tamer?

212   WYR be a social media influencer or a community hero?

213   WYR look young when you're desperate to be older or look your age when you want to be younger?

214   WYR give or take bad advice?

215   WYR live forever but look your age or always look young but live an average length of life?

216   WYR have the grace of a swan or the memory of an elephant?

217   WYR have your decisions made for you by other people or by tossing a coin?

218   WYR lose all the photos on your smartphone or lose your tickets for the big game?

219   WYR have ears that can record what you hear or eyes that can record what you see?

220   WYR be a flightless bird or a non-venomous snake?

221   WYR have a frozen shoulder or be given the cold shoulder?

222   WYR be able to pause time once a day or go back ten seconds once a day at will?

223   WYR eat what you want and never be overweight or never exercise and always be fit?

224   WYR have a personal robot or a flying carpet?

225   WYR have more time or more money?

226   WYR be able to change the length of your hair at will or snap your fingers to change outfits?

227   WYR meet a superhero or a cartoon character?

228   WYR have a bugle fanfare as you enter a room or a drum roll before you speak?

229 WYR kiss a dirty trashcan or a frog?

230 WYR brush your teeth with soap or curdled milk?

231 WYR know the lyrics to every song or know the moves to every dance?

232 WYR have one puppy or five kittens?

233 WYR be a maid for the untidiest person in the world or a chef for the fussiest eater in the world?

234 WYR have a magic button that could stop other people from talking or stop other people from moving?

235 WYR never feel pain or have your loved ones never feel pain?

236 WYR have crooked white teeth or straight yellow-stained teeth?

237 WYR have five cavities or five warts?

238 WYR see something no one else can see or not see something everyone else can see?

239 WYR be able to see smells or smell sounds?

240   WYR be able to sketch things into existence or erase existing things with an eraser?

241   WYR have the power to push things away using your eyes or pull things toward you using your eyes?

242   WYR accidentally spoil a movie for someone or have someone spoil a movie for you?

243   WYR walk on your hands or eat with your feet?

244   WYR have a private paradise island or a private amusement park?

245   WYR live one long life of a thousand years or live ten different lives, each lasting a hundred years?

246   WYR please others or please yourself?

247   WYR have the power to shrink everything at will or make things double in size?

248   WYR trip and fall running toward someone or running away from someone?

249   WYR be the first person to explore a planet or be the inventor of a drug that cures a deadly disease?

250 WYR be the last to know good news or the first to know bad news?

251 WYR look like a magazine front-cover model or be totally comfortable in your own skin?

252 WYR use your non-dominant hand to write or to eat?

253 WYR never get tired or never have to go to the bathroom?

254 WYR grow new teeth like a shark or wear down your constantly growing teeth like a beaver?

255 WYR teleport to a different dimension or to a different country in this dimension?

256 WYR be the superhero or the superhero's indispensable sidekick?

257 WYR be bulletproof or have the power to catch bullets in your hands?

258 WYR be able to fly on a broomstick or have an invisibility cloak?

259 WYR have a dog's brain in a human body or a human brain in a dog's body?

260   WYR never be sad again or never be angry again?

261   WYR love animals but be allergic to them or not be allergic to animals but be frightened of them?

262   WYR never be rejected ever again or never fail ever again?

263   WYR have a time machine or a teleport machine?

264   WYR be totally alone for a year or never be alone for a year?

265   WYR win an Academy Award or an Olympic medal?

266   WYR figure things out for yourself or ask for help?

267   WYR cry tears of lemonade or sneeze cheese?

268   WYR be true to yourself or fake it till you make it?

269   WYR lie to your family or lie to your friends?

270   WYR argue until the cows come home or walk away from an argument?

271   WYR get caught in a swarm of crickets or an army of ants?

272   WYR own a restaurant chain or a hotel chain?

273   WYR have a broken foot or a broken hand?

274   WYR spill a pot of silver glitter on a black carpet or a pot of paprika on a white carpet?

275   WYR go back to age five with everything you know now or know now everything your future self will learn?

276   WYR a movie was made of your life since the age of twenty-one or before the age of twenty-one?

277   WYR never be able to ask another question or never be able to answer another question?

278   WYR read everything out loud or speak your thoughts out loud?

279   WYR do a TED talk or sing a song on stage at a concert with your favorite singer?

280   WYR lose three friends or gain an enemy?

281 WYR end crime or end poverty?

282 WYR wake up and be unable to see your reflection in a mirror or not recognize the person you see in the mirror?

283 WYR have it all or know it all?

284 WYR lose your wallet or lose all the photos on your phone?

285 WYR never move from the house you grew up in or move into a different house every two years?

286 WYR own a dragon or be a dragon?

287 WYR hold a grudge or let bygones be bygones?

288 WYR sit through a movie you're not enjoying or pay for a meal you're not enjoying?

289 WYR be a real-world magician or a wizard in a fantasy world?

290 WYR have a missing finger or an extra toe?

291 WYR go to prison for your best friend's crime or have your best friend go to prison for your crime?

292   WYR everyone had to backflip into meeting rooms or cartwheel out of meeting rooms?

293   WYR have a suitcase full of dollars or a blood-stained knife in your car when pulled over by a police officer?

294   WYR misread everything you read or mispronounce everything you say?

295   WYR get eggs fresh from your own chickens or milk fresh from your own cow?

296   WYR never be credited or take the credit for someone else's efforts?

297   WYR be reincarnated as a bee or a tree?

298   WYR speak in rhyme or speak in riddles?

299   WYR have first pick or have the last laugh?

300   WYR be held in high regard by your parents or your friends?

301   WYR be happy and you know it or be beautiful and not know it?

302 WYR have a wolf at the door or not be able to get your foot in the door?

303 WYR make an entrance or pussyfoot around?

304 WYR have a flying carpet or a car that can drive underwater?

305 WYR have a bad taste in your mouth or smell a bit funky?

306 WYR be snug as a bug in a rug or cool as a cucumber?

307 WYR get your way or go with the flow?

308 WYR be an average person in the present or a king of a large country 2500 years ago?

309 WYR have the power to control your dreams or control the dreams of others?

310 WYR have a pet that can talk to you (only you) or a pet that never dies?

311 WYR have an invisibility cloak or a spaceship with a cloaking device?

312 WYR be a space pirate or an eighteenth-century smuggler?

313 WYR be feared by all or loved by all?

314 WYR only be able to eat when it's dark outside or only be able to sleep when it's light outside?

315 WYR live in a world with no crime or no lies?

316 WYR be forgetful or clumsy?

317 WYR play baseball with a basketball or football with a tennis ball?

318 WYR a story you're writing became reality or a story you're reading became reality?

319 WYR have fangs or a crooked smile?

320 WYR clean a public restroom without gloves or walk through a cow field without socks and shoes?

321 WYR be able to see five minutes into the future or five years into the future?

322   WYR have unshakeable will power or have a credit card with no limit?

323   WYR become a ghost or a zombie when you die?

324   WYR be obsessive and meticulous or haphazard and nonchalant?

325   WYR be feared or be fearless?

326   WYR sweep things under the rug or risk opening a can of worms?

327   WYR never have to barf again or never have constipation ever again?

328   WYR spend the day in a beautiful location on a rainy day or a dull location on a sunny day?

329   WYR wake up as a giant cockroach or a giant snail?

330   WYR spend a day washing glass windows or wearing glass shoes?

331   WYR have the eyes of a painting follow you around a room or be secretly filmed by a hidden camera?

332   WYR love or be loved?

333 WYR hug or fist bump?

334 WYR all food looked the same or tasted the same?

335 WYR be liked or be respected?

336 WYR paint the town red or be tickled pink?

337 WYR be a free spirit or know your sole purpose in life?

338 WYR be poor but help people or become rich by hurting people?

339 WYR do whatever it takes or have the moral high ground?

340 WYR be tongue-tied or be a blabbermouth?

341 WYR have greater intelligence or greater wisdom?

342 WYR experience being your ninety-year-old self or return to being your nine-year-old self for a day?

343 WYR surprise someone by baking them a cake or have someone surprise you by jumping out of a cake?

344   WYR be the queen bee or king of the hill?

345   WYR have a song written about you or have your life story written?

346   WYR kiss a jellyfish or shake hands with your worst enemy?

347   WYR be able to change the world or just change the way your life panned out in the last year?

348   WYR have bulging eyes or bow legs?

349   WYR know the true meaning of love or the meaning of life?

350   WYR do things right or do the right thing?

351   WYR there was only one global language or everyone had to be multilingual?

352   WYR have more time or more power?

353   WYR live under a sky with no stars at night or live under a sky with no clouds during the day?

354   WYR have high self-esteem or always have a shoulder to cry on?

355 WYR never be embarrassed again or never cry again?

356 WYR already have everything you want or be able to afford anything you want?

357 WYR never cheat or cheat only if you knew you couldn't be found out?

358 WYR fall madly in love with everyone you meet or feel deeply suspicious of everyone you meet?

359 WYR have great mental health but poor physical health or great physical health but poor mental health?

360 WYR be responsible for sending an innocent person to prison or for letting a guilty person go free?

361 WYR never have to clean a bathroom again or never have to do dishes again?

362 WYR trust your intuition or trust the opinions of friends and family?

363 WYR have superficial knowledge of most things or a deep knowledge of a few things?

364 WYR settle for what you already know or keep on asking more questions?

365 WYR live ten more years with excellent health or live thirty more years with declining health?

366 WYR be left alone when you're feeling down or have someone cheer you up?

367 WYR never be brokenhearted or never break someone's heart?

368 WYR walk in the moonlight or run in the sun?

369 WYR cry crocodile tears or cry wolf?

370 WYR be where you are now or be anywhere other than where you are now?

371 WYR super-sensitive taste or super-sensitive hearing?

372 WYR learn the hard way or never make a mistake?

373 WYR do what you love or love what you're doing?

374 WYR sell all of your possessions or sell one of your organs?

375 WYR relive yesterday just as it was or relive it to change it?

376 WYR your shirts were two sizes too big or one size too small?

377 WYR know when it's time to give in and let go or never quit?

378 WYR lose your mojo or lose your marbles?

379 WYR be more like your mom or more like your dad?

380 WYR be able to remember every dream or forget every nightmare?

381 WYR never experience loneliness or never have your trust broken?

382 WYR swap lives with your favorite celebrity or a character from a book you've read?

383 WYR buy things on impulse or write a shopping list and stick to it?

384 WYR keep the name you have or permanently change your name?

385 WYR keep your own secret or keep a friend's secret for life?

386 WYR be a male midwife or a female construction worker?

387 WYR go back on your word or eat your words?

388 WYR write someone a love letter or confess how you feel
face to face?

389 WYR believe in fate or believe that nothing happens unless you
make it happen?

390 WYR never be able to smell your favorite scent again or never
smell the aroma of your favorite food again?

391 WYR never be hated or never be wrong?

392 WYR never be annoyed by anyone ever again or never lose your
patience ever again?

393 WYR be rewarded for an act of heroism or for winning an
international competition?

394 WYR relive a year of your life or have no memories of a year
in your life?

395 WYR be unpopular or be popular for doing something you're
not proud of?

396   WYR stick with tradition or never be governed by any tradition?

397   WYR play a board game or a video game?

398   WYR treat yourself by eating your favorite dessert or by buying a new item of clothing?

399   WYR have an evening out at a comedy club or in a nightclub?

400   WYR trip and fall as you step up to give a presentation or forget what you're saying halfway through a presentation?

401   WYR become a millionaire or get to live in the fictional world of your favorite movie?

402   WYR die in twenty years with no regrets or die in fifty with many regrets?

403   WYR hear voices in your head or see dead people?

404   WYR have no sense of humor or no sense of danger?

405   WYR be agoraphobic or a germaphobe?

406   WYR have the most beautiful eyes or the most amazing smile?

407 WYR have a horrible job, but be able to retire comfortably in ten years or have your dream job, but work until you die?

408 WYR be a garbage collector or a celebrity whom people love to hate?

409 WYR know what the future holds for you or know what the future holds for your family members?

410 WYR live a nomadic lifestyle or settle in one place?

411 WYR have political power but be poor or be rich but have no political power?

412 WYR party hard every night or never party again?

413 WYR have a secret lair or a private jet?

414 WYR be covered in hair or be completely bald?

415 WYR never feel guilty again or never feel awkward again?

416 WYR have the power to wipe an annoying celebrity you can't stand from existence or a band?

417 WYR be able to punch someone in the face and get away with it or pretend to be someone else and get away with it?

418 WYR keep money you found in a taxi or give it to the taxi driver?

419 WYR it was the day after tomorrow or the day before yesterday?

420 WYR be the person you are today or become a different version of you?

421 WYR sleep an hour less than you need or go to bed an hour too early?

422 WYR meet your doppelgänger or meet the doppelgänger of someone you know?

423 WYR be a sleepwalker or a sleep talker?

424 WYR never make fun of someone ever again or never have others poke fun at you?

425 WYR have an alien friend or an invisible friend?

426 WYR stop to smell the flowers or be a rolling stone that gathers no moss?

427 WYR have your worst enemy read your diary or have all the pictures on your phone posted online?

428 WYR never see your best friend again or never see your pet again?

429 WYR have friends who are more attractive than you or smarter than you?

430 WYR be the person who prevented a war or the person who ended a war?

431 WYR have a weird laugh or a weird sense of humor?

432 WYR have tentacles instead of arms or instead of legs?

433 WYR have a gap between your front teeth or pointed ears?

434 WYR be chased by an angry bee or an agitated seagull?

435 WYR be sixteen forever or thirty-five forever?

436 WYR volunteer in an animal shelter or at a children's home?

437 WYR never be able to watch football again or never be able to shoot hoops again?

438   WYR drink a glass of vinegar or eat a block of butter?

439   WYR never read a book again or never go bowling again?

440   WYR switch bodies with the person on your right or switch heads with the person on your left?

441   WYR only be able to wear purple for a month or only be able to eat white-colored foods for a week?

442   WYR pretend you're sick to get out of going somewhere or pretend to get a call to get out of a conversation?

443   WYR be out of your depth or out of time?

444   WYR live in a world with no evil people or a world with no disease?

445   WYR keep your finger on the pulse or let the world pass you by?

446   WYR climb the corporate ladder or climb trees?

447   WYR learn how to dance the fandango or learn how to cook a soufflé?

448   WYR have a lifetime supply of shampoo or breakfast cereal?

449 WYR have a career mentor or a life coach?

450 WYR go to a family reunion or a school reunion?

451 WYR have family you consider friends or friends you consider family?

452 WYR direct a movie or star in a movie?

453 WYR get it right the first time every time or be given a second chance every time?

454 WYR read a newspaper or watch the news on TV?

455 WYR take over the family business or start your own business?

456 WYR be a cancer survivor or the lone survivor of a train wreck?

457 WYR drink iced coffee in the winter or hot chocolate in the summer?

458 WYR change something about yourself or change something about the world?

459 WYR be able to have a conversation with your favorite stuffed animal or with people in paintings?

460 WYR look at the stars in the night sky or listen to waves lapping on the shore?

461 WYR be a master impersonator or a master ventriloquist?

462 WYR be free as a bird or happy as a lark?

463 WYR pretend to be into something you're not to impress someone or pretend not to like something you do?

464 WYR help a loved one cover up a crime or give up your beloved pet if a loved one became allergic?

465 WYR never look stupid or never take yourself too seriously?

466 WYR be right but resented by others or wrong and constantly reminded of it by others?

467 WYR be lonely on your own or lonely in a crowd?

468 WYR die a horrible death or eat a part of your body to survive?

469 WYR live in a world with no electricity or no animals?

470 WYR stick by the belief that honesty is the best policy or that nice guys finish last?

471 WYR become uglier as you age or dumber as you age?

472 WYR share an apartment with a neat freak or a slob?

473 WYR stink or have everybody else stink except you?

474 WYR have your parents embarrass you or be a disappointment to your parents?

475 WYR listen to a ten-minute drum solo or a ten-minute banjo solo?

476 WYR be caught dancing in your underwear or caught licking your plate?

477 WYR dance with someone who has no natural rhythm or sing with someone who is tone deaf?

478 WYR have a friend who never pays their share or a friend who keeps asking to borrow money?

479 WYR be told you're too serious or you're too ridiculous?

480 WYR read a book containing poor grammar or one with a weak plotline?

481 WYR be unable to say any words beginning with D or any words beginning with R?

482 WYR wear wrinkled clothes or wear dirty shoes?

483 WYR everyone in the world suddenly became much younger than you or much older than you?

484 WYR own up to making a mistake or own up to telling a lie?

485 WYR be a zombie slayer or a tooth fairy?

486 WYR be an Olympic athlete or a Hollywood actor?

487 WYR be insane and know you're insane or insane and believe you're sane?

488 WYR be featured on the front page of *The New York Times* or *Sports Illustrated*?

489 WYR be in a globally famous band popular with kindergarten kids or be in an obscure rock band?

490 WYR dress like a rapper or dress like a rockabilly?

491 WYR have your house blown down by the big bad wolf or carried away by a twister?

492 WYR never be able to say "please" or never be able to say "thank you"?

493 WYR be wanted or needed?

494 WYR be on trend or dare to be different and set your own style?

495 WYR be trapped in a sandstorm or caught in quicksand?

496 WYR be a child star actor who fails as an adult actor or a one-hit wonder in the music industry?

497 WYR never have a dream come true or have your biggest dream *and* your worst nightmare come true?

498 WYR learn how to read again or learn how to walk again?

499 WYR visit a unicorn petting zoo or a dragon ride park?

500 WYR spend a weekend with a paranoid person or someone who has just been dumped?

501 WYR live for a year without money or without electricity?

502 WYR be a boy mistaken for a girl or a girl mistaken for a boy?

503 WYR give up potatoes or pasta?

504 WYR be able to catch flies with your tongue like a frog or swivel your eyes like a chameleon?

505 WYR have two left hands or two left feet?

506 WYR slow down to walk with someone or have to jog to keep up with them?

507 WYR go caving or mountain climbing?

508 WYR go on a protest march or start an online petition?

509 WYR be in a relationship with someone ten years older or ten years younger than you?

510   WYR break a bone or chip a tooth?

511   WYR be a hitchhiker or pick up a hitchhiker?

512   WYR never be fired from your job or never be questioned by a police officer?

513   WYR be nominated for an Oscar ten times and never win or win on your first nomination and never be nominated again?

514   WYR be the only fairy that can't fly or the elf that's twice the size of the other elves?

515   WYR be a false alibi for a friend or let a friend be jailed for something they didn't do?

516   WYR get the highest score or make the longest word in a game of Scrabble?

517   WYR lie in a job interview or use a fake ID?

518   WYR be a vegetarian with a meat-eating partner or a meat-eater with a vegetarian partner?

519   WYR be an amazing painter or a brilliant mathematician?

520 WYR never lose your phone again or never lose your keys again?

521 WYR disappoint a family member or a friend?

522 WYR dye your hair and regret it or tell someone you love them and not mean it?

523 WYR brush your teeth with a hairbrush or comb your hair with a fork?

524 WYR have chapped lips that never heal or terrible dandruff that can't be treated?

525 WYR instantly change the color of your hair or the length of your hair?

526 WYR have been the first person to reach the North Pole or the first person to climb Mount Everest?

527 WYR be caught kissing your reflection or kissing a photo of a celebrity?

528 WYR never be in a car accident or never be in handcuffs?

529 WYR miss a deadline or miss a payment?

530   WYR get up early to get a job done or stay up late to get a job done?

531   WYR vomit in a taxi or pee your pants in a taxi?

532   WYR know when you're going to die or how you're going to die?

533   WYR have unlimited sushi for life or unlimited tacos for life?

534   WYR accidentally break a piece of furniture by sitting on it or accidentally break a window?

535   WYR be shouted at by a customer or by your boss?

536   WYR break up with someone in public or have someone break up with you by text?

537   WYR be able to shed your skin like a snake or regrow a missing limb like a salamander?

538   WYR find a hair in your food or a fly in your drink?

539   WYR be blown over by the wind or knocked off your feet by a wave?

540 WYR never get a speeding ticket or never get carded?

541 WYR get something stuck up your nose or in your ear?

542 WYR meet a mermaid or an elf?

543 WYR do a tandem bungee jump or a tandem skydive?

544 WYR know how to milk a cow or lasso a calf?

545 WYR not be able to see any colors or have mild but constant tinnitus (ringing in the ears)?

546 WYR have constantly dry eyes or a constant runny nose?

547 WYR know the history of every object you touched or be able to talk to animals?

548 WYR be kept alive for years on life support or be allowed to die?

549 WYR be forced to eat only spicy food or only incredibly bland food?

550 WYR have a life-changing adventure or be able to stop time?

551 WYR travel first class and stay in a budget hotel or travel budget class and stay in a five-star hotel?

552 WYR be responsible for the death of a child or for the deaths of three adults?

553 WYR have a pet jellyfish or a pet stick insect?

554 WYR meet the author of your favorite book or be able to meet a character from the book?

555 WYR go to jail for four years for something you didn't do or get away with something you did but live in fear of being caught?

556 WYR play video games for twelve hours nonstop or watch movies for twelve hours nonstop?

557 WYR only ever have one hairstyle and no bad hair days or have the option to try lots of different styles?

558 WYR never be sweaty again or never get dirty again?

559 WYR get free tickets to a theme park or a water park?

560 WYR be an extra in an Oscar-winning movie or the lead in a box office bomb?

561 WYR have a crooked nose from a sports injury or a cauliflower ear?

562 WYR cook a meal blindfolded or eat a meal with your hands tied behind your back?

563 WYR be able to balance a spoon on the end of your nose or touch your nose with your tongue?

564 WYR win a staring contest or an arm-wrestling match?

565 WYR be known as the life and soul of the party or the go-to person in an emergency?

566 WYR always be overdressed or always underdressed?

567 WYR get an animal-image tattoo or have a tattoo of someone's name?

568 WYR have a secret family recipe or a family heirloom?

569 WYR have seven sons or seven daughters?

570 WYR be immune to physical pain or have no emotions?

571 WYR be a logical thinker or be considered a bit of a space cadet?

572 WYR be lucky in love or talented in your career?

573 WYR be famous for pulling off an audacious heist or a daring jailbreak?

574 WYR be the record producer who turned down The Beatles or the publisher who rejected J.K. Rowling?

575 WYR be the second choice of your first love or be the first choice of your second love?

576 WYR cheat death or cheat on a partner?

577 WYR socialize with mega-rich entrepreneurs or famous musicians?

578 WYR love your face but not your body or love your body but not your face?

579 WYR be the defense attorney for a guilty person or the prosecution against an innocent person?

580 WYR share an office with a narcissist or a sociopath?

581 WYR be malnourished or dehydrated?

582 WYR hire a sixteen-year-old babysitter or a seventy-six-year-old babysitter?

583 WYR spend time doing it yourself to save money or spend money on having someone else do it to save time?

584 WYR choose truth or dare?

585 WYR take the blame to get your best friend out of trouble or take credit for something to get your worst enemy into trouble?

586 WYR only be able to see one color or smell one smell?

587 WYR hear a growl behind you or a scream ahead of you when you're alone in the woods?

588 WYR be able to live someone else's life for fifteen minutes or read someone's thoughts for fifteen minutes?

589 WYR own a cat with a human face or a dog with human hands for paws?

590 WYR have a fear of a duck watching you (anatidaephobia) or fear of the color yellow (xanthophobia)?

591 WYR be able to revive plants with your tears or kill weeds with your laughter?

592 WYR be armed with a banjo or an egg whisk in a zombie attack?

593 WYR work behind the scenes at The White House or work behind the scenes in Hollywood?

594 WYR be able to custom-make your ideal partner or your ideal family?

595 WYR have freckles on your nose or a dimple on your chin?

596 WYR be accused of being a spendthrift or a miser?

597 WYR meet a dinosaur or an alien?

598 WYR never get lost or never lose your balance?

599 WYR reveal your deepest fear or your secret crush?

600 WYR lick the floor or lick food retrieved from a trash can?

601 WYR be the opposite sex for a month or work the night shift for a month?

602 WYR be caught sucking your thumb or sleeping with a stuffed toy?

603 WYR hurt someone by telling a lie or by saying something mean?

604 WYR keep a smile on your face all day or get through a day without laughing?

605 WYR never lose your memory or never lose your eyesight?

606 WYR have your most disgusting (and secret) habit discovered or be arrested by police and taken in for questioning?

607 WYR hold a live insect in your mouth for ten seconds or have rats walk over you for ten seconds?

608 WYR never feel envy again or never feel vengeful again?

609 WYR find a skunk in your bed or a goose in your shower?

610 WYR switch socks with the person on your left or switch tops with the person on your right?

611 WYR have all your clothes fit perfectly or have the most comfortable pillow, blankets, and sheets in existence?

612 WYR take part in a twenty-four-hour dance-a-thon or a twenty-four-hour cook-a-thon?

613 WYR be considered vain or plain?

614 WYR put relationships over career or put your career first?

615 WYR be considered aggressive or a pushover?

616 WYR know how to pick a lock or how to hotwire a car?

617 WYR feel free or safe?

618 WYR be a member of your favorite band for a day or be transported into your favorite game for a day?

619 WYR never be able to talk to anyone again or never be able to touch anyone again?

620 WYR work in waste disposal or bomb disposal?

621 WYR slip and fall in a puddle of vomit or get sprayed by a skunk?

622 WYR see the creation of the universe or the end of the universe?

623 WYR lack imagination or lack subtlety?

624   WYR eat a handful of hair or drink a cup of spit?

625   WYR only be able to eat green vegetables or red fruit?

626   WYR be able to clear the world's oceans of plastic or save the rainforests?

627   WYR live with a dog that snores loudly or a partner who talks in their sleep?

628   WYR lose a day of your life every time you swear or every time you say something mean?

629   WYR hang out with the first person you ever had a crush on or the first person you ever dated?

630   WYR be proactive or procrastinate?

631   WYR be able to do a split or do a backflip?

632   WYR have free internet for life or free food for life?

633   WYR give a colleague a piggyback around your workplace for a day or be given piggybacks all day?

634 WYR be a skilled whistler or a skilled spoons player?

635 WYR have bad breath or smelly feet?

636 WYR have eyes that can film everything or ears that can record all sound?

637 WYR paint a picture or paint a garden fence?

638 WYR switch places with a spider or a mouse?

639 WYR have three eyes or a tail?

640 WYR be trapped in a room with walls moving in or tied to a post with water levels rising?

641 WYR wake up to a snake or a bear in your bedroom?

642 WYR have your car written off in a car crash or lose all your files in a computer crash?

643 WYR find $50 or be hugged?

644 WYR live in a country with a low cost of living but horrible weather or live in a country with a high cost of living and amazing weather?

645 WYR be a world-renowned photographer or a world-renowned animal trainer?

646 WYR feel brave or feel smart?

647 WYR share everything in your life with others or keep it all to yourself?

648 WYR understand how animals communicate or the laws of quantum mechanics?

649 WYR be able to successfully grow anything you want in the yard or be an accomplished classical musician?

650 WYR tell a stranger their underwear was showing or look the other way?

651 WYR have money and no love or love and no money?

652 WYR have great wisdom or good health?

653 WYR marry a poor person from your culture or a rich person from a different culture?

654 WYR be able to touch your toes without bending your knees or rub your tummy and pat your head?

655   WYR have no nose or no ears?

656   WYR be woken up by an air horn every morning or do a four-mile run on waking every morning?

657   WYR meet a mini hippo or a giant wasp?

658   WYR be the apple of someone's eye or be someone with a finger in every pie?

659   WYR work alone in the day or work with colleagues on the night shift?

660   WYR ask a loaded question or shoot from the hip when answering a question?

661   WYR let sleeping dogs lie or let the cat out of the bag?

662   WYR drink warm soda or eat cold curry?

663   WYR be a skilled architect or a skilled graphic designer?

664   WYR go gray naturally as you age or dye your hair to cover gray as you age?

665 WYR go ghost hunting or storm chasing?

666 WYR have super-sharp reflexes or be super flexible?

667 WYR wear entirely neon pink or entirely plaid?

668 WYR be one of a kind or one of the in-crowd?

669 WYR be hated or be a hater?

670 WYR be in a long-distance relationship or be married to someone in the military?

671 WYR be rich and famous or just rich?

672 WYR be sophisticated and aloof or be the boy/girl next door and gregarious?

673 WYR learn to communicate using Morse code or semaphore flag signals?

674 WYR eat green apples or red grapes?

675 WYR go without your phone or go without food for two days?

676   WYR have lunch with a friend or dinner with colleagues?

677   WYR be the child of celebrity parents or have a famous sibling?

678   WYR have a DJ or a live band at your party?

679   WYR be a legendary adventurer or a legendary performer?

680   WYR go sugar-free or gluten-free?

681   WYR stay in bed all day or stay awake all night?

682   WYR move to a new city or town every week or never be able to leave the city or town you were born in?

683   WYR camp for a night with a stranger or camp for a night alone?

684   WYR work for an angry boss or work in an environment that makes you angry?

685   WYR save an antique painting or your favorite shoes from a fire?

686   WYR be able to undo every mistake you ever made or never make another mistake going forward?

687   WYR have charisma or great hair?

688   WYR be alone on Valentine's Day or alone on New Year's Eve?

689   WYR have a cut on your lip or a canker sore on your tongue?

690   WYR be blackmailed or wear chain mail?

691   WYR be held hostage for six months or go into hiding for six months?

692   WYR be surrounded by people who brag nonstop about their great life or people who moan nonstop about their unfair life?

693   WYR do an outdoor job in pouring rain or under a baking hot sun?

694   WYR pull out one of your own teeth or stitch up your own arm?

695   WYR lose all the photographs you've taken this year or all the photographs of you in your childhood?

696   WYR have four arms or two mouths?

697   WYR share a cab with someone who has bad breath or someone with body odor?

698   WYR meet the real Easter bunny or the real Santa?

699   WYR fall out of bed or fall off a bench?

700   WYR end racism or end sexism?

701   WYR plunge into ice-cold water or chug a glass of ice-cold water?

702   WYR lose the last piece of your 2,000-piece jigsaw or lose a card from your deck?

703   WYR never play your favorite sport again or lose whenever you play?

704   WYR have a completely automated home or a self-driving car?

705   WYR be blocked by someone on social media or be ghosted?

706   WYR break the law or break both your arms?

707   WYR cry for no reason or laugh for no reason?

708   WYR be a hip-hop superstar or hula hoop superstar?

709 WYR have an overly possessive partner or an overly needy pet?

710 WYR be a roofer with a fear of heights or a coal miner with a fear of small spaces?

711 WYR have a romantic dinner or a romantic slow dance?

712 WYR be transported into a medieval banquet or a Roman feast?

713 WYR have a traditional wedding or get married in Las Vegas?

714 WYR only need to sleep for one night each week or only need to eat one meal each week?

715 WYR be able to complete a one-week project in one day or complete two one-week projects in one week?

716 WYR be a bounty hunter or a bargain hunter?

717 WYR wear a neck brace for a month or have braces on your teeth for two months?

718 WYR be on the outside looking in or be an outlier?

719 WYR only be able to read the first half of any book or watch the second half of any movie?

720 WYR ask a question no one wants to answer or give an answer no one wants to hear?

721 WYR decorate your home all in red or wear only red?

722 WYR be able to change the way your hair parts or change the shape of your eyebrows at will?

723 WYR your hair turned green in direct sunlight or your skin turned green when wet?

724 WYR have a job on an assembly line or a supermarket checkout?

725 WYR be able to change the length of your hair by pushing your belly button or have a prehensile ponytail?

726 WYR be chased by hyenas or hippos?

727 WYR be on a long bus journey with twenty Elvis impersonators or twenty mime artists?

728 WYR settle an argument with a break-dancing contest or a bake-off?

729   WYR be able to adjust your height by twiddling your earlobe or change your hairstyle by pushing your nose?

730   WYR have paws instead of hands or hooves instead of feet?

731   WYR sleep hanging upside down like a bat or sleep standing up like a giraffe?

732   WYR feel compelled to follow everything you say with an evil laugh or begin every sentence with "Simon says . . ."?

733   WYR tell people you come from a galaxy far, far away or you come from a land that time forgot?

734   WYR be stuck on a desert island with a basketball or a Rubik's Cube?

735   WYR have an extreme phobia of trees and flowers or of people named after trees and flowers?

736   WYR have your strength determined by the length of your hair or your intelligence by the length of your fingers?

737   WYR be able to play your fingers like panpipes or your thighs like bongos?

738 WYR be able to choose the weather each day or choose how many hours you spend at work each day?

739 WYR be able to style your hair by thinking about it or wash and dry your clothes by dancing around them?

740 WYR be the author of *101 Things to Do with a Stick* or *101 Meals to Make with Kale*?

741 WYR win the Nobel Prize in Physics or be a noble knight with a trusty steed?

742 WYR be locked overnight in a museum or an amusement park?

743 WYR be a storm in a teacup or be the eye of a storm?

744 WYR enter an Elvis impersonator contest or the rock-paper-scissors world championships?

745 WYR have three wheels on your wagon or be three sheets to the wind?

746 WYR be one person's favorite person or be a fan favorite?

747 WYR listen to the sound of a breeze in the trees or bacon sizzling?

748 WYR have your eye on the prize or play it by ear?

749 WYR win the lottery and die the next day or get a free ride when you've already paid?

750 WYR spend a rainy afternoon playing Uno with family or playing *Animal Crossing* alone?

751 WYR re-read a book or re-watch a movie?

752 WYR only be able to wash your hair three times a year or check your phone three times a week?

753 WYR be the President of the United States for a day or a billionaire for a day?

754 WYR hold your horses or be like a bat out of hell?

755 WYR have your face suddenly become pixelated or your voice suddenly become disguised on a first date?

756 WYR watch lambs skipping in a meadow or fish jumping in a pond?

757 WYR be an Englishman in New York or a New Yorker in London?

758   WYR be accused of being too optimistic or too pessimistic?

759   WYR have a permanent itch on your nose or a permanently sweaty left foot?

760   WYR be Zoom-bombed during an important video conference or be unable to turn off the cat-face filter?

761   WYR only listen to sad songs or not listen to music at all?

762   WYR be able to buy top-ups for emotions or buy upgrades for broken hearts?

763   WYR use popular catchphrases from TV shows or create your own?

764   WYR have barely legible handwriting but great typing skills or have beautiful handwriting and only be able to type with two fingers?

765   WYR take a quick shower or a long bath?

766   WYR always wear socks or never wear socks?

767   WYR have all your debt canceled or be free from all allergies?

768 WYR see a biographical movie of your favorite singer or read your favorite actor's autobiography?

769 WYR stick with your favorite brand or get paid to give your opinion on new brands?

770 WYR only own the few things you need or own lots of things even if you never use them?

771 WYR never lose anything again or never lose your temper?

772 WYR be able to wiggle your ears or curl your tongue?

773 WYR be able to shrink your car to pocketsize when you're not driving or supersize yourself at will?

774 WYR do the job you do now or be able to snap your fingers and have the skills you need to change jobs?

775 WYR trade places with a person or an animal?

776 WYR be able to ask your past self a single question or ask your future self a single question?

777 WYR be a talented liar or a talented lie detector?

778   WYR be a bookworm or go on a wormhole adventure?

779   WYR live in virtual reality where you are all-powerful or live in the real world and be able to go anywhere but not be able to interact with anyone or anything?

780   WYR write a book or be the subject of a book?

781   WYR look the same at forty as you did at twenty or look the same at eighty as you did at forty?

782   WYR have someone tell you that you're smart or you're funny?

783   WYR have eyebrows that can crawl around your face or hair that can fly away at random intervals?

784   WYR take a daily bath with a friendly hippo or go for a daily jog with a friendly emu?

785   WYR be in the crow's nest on a ship in a sea storm or in an elevator when an earthquake strikes?

786   WYR ban fake tanning products or guyliner (eyeliner for men)?

787   WYR look down your nose or put your foot in your mouth?

788 WYR eat food through your fingertips or breathe through your elbows?

789 WYR see feelings or feel sounds?

790 WYR follow the instructions or throw caution to the wind?

791 WYR be a high diver who forgets how to swim or a racing driver who forgets how to drive?

792 WYR be able to give change for a dollar by putting it in your mouth or be able to breathe fire?

793 WYR have a bird in the hand or two in the bush?

794 WYR have six fingers on your left hand or three fingers on your right hand?

795 WYR use mustard instead of hair gel or salad dressing instead of shower gel?

796 WYR have been the first person to walk on the moon or be the first person to walk on Mars?

797 WYR have the final say on who gets to star in movies or have control over who wins sporting championships?

798   WYR eat to live or live to eat?

799   WYR be a master at the art of origami or macramé?

800   WYR inherit personality traits from your parents or your grandparents?

801   WYR have a magic compass that can lead you to anywhere you want to go or lead you to whatever you want to find?

802   WYR be a one-eared rabbit or a one-eyed mouse?

803   WYR travel the world for a year with all expenses paid or have $500,000 to spend on whatever you want?

804   WYR step barefoot on a sea urchin or grab a thistle with bare hands?

805   WYR have a perfect day or a perfect evening?

806   WYR be late for a meeting at work or late the first time you meet your partner's parents?

807   WYR have the world's biggest collection of sports memorabilia or army tanks?

808 WYR have the job of winding up the clocks in a clock museum or cleaning the mirrors in a hall of mirrors?

809 WYR be like a fish out of water or be in hot water?

810 WYR face your biggest fear for $1 million or do a picked-at-random dare for $2 million?

811 WYR be able to control fire or water?

812 WYR be a sight for sore eyes or catch someone's eye?

813 WYR be caught in an unexpected location or caught doing something surprising?

814 WYR make one gargantuan decision right now or make one big decision every year with a coin toss?

815 WYR offer a friend career advice or personal advice?

816 WYR see the first artist you saw in concert again or the last artist you saw in concert?

817 WYR play two truths and a lie or charades?

818 WYR be able to go back and change something your parents did or go back and change something you said to your parents?

819 WYR get a tattoo of the pet you dreamed of having when you were five or of the person on your left?

820 WYR be able to erase a year in your life (unlive it) or erase three people (unmeet them)?

821 WYR relive the best party you ever went to or the best family outing you ever went on?

822 WYR be tested on your spelling ability right now or your math ability right now?

823 WYR be able to buy one object, no matter the price, or meet one person (dead or alive)?

824 WYR be able to choose the gender of your unborn baby or their physical features?

825 WYR have written a play or had an article published in a magazine?

826 WYR take ballet lessons to become more graceful or take up rowing to improve your stamina?

827 WYR not be able to swim or not be able to ride a bicycle?

828 WYR be able to hold your breath for two minutes or run a mile in under seven minutes?

829 WYR only eat raw potato or only ever eat cooked (never raw) tomatoes?

830 WYR only cook once each week or only cook with a deep fryer?

831 WYR not be able to whistle or not be able to snap your fingers?

832 WYR be tired no matter how much you sleep or constantly hungry no matter how much you eat?

833 WYR never use a public restroom or never give a speech in public?

834 WYR spend fifteen minutes trying to catch a fly or spend fifteen minutes on hold on the phone?

835 WYR play the harmonica or sing a cappella?

836 WYR take part in a mud wrestling contest or make a Mississippi mud pie?

837 WYR go ice fishing or learn how to make ice sculptures?

838 WYR always go to bed before 10 pm or always eat chocolate chip pancakes for breakfast?

839 WYR spend two years with your soulmate before they die, leaving you to never love again, or spend your life with someone nice you settled for?

840 WYR never break a bone or never break a promise?

841 WYR be able to play a guitar with your teeth or behind your back?

842 WYR be able to touch your nose with your tongue or play the flute with your nose?

843 WYR have a fear of anything that jumps or anything that beeps?

844 WYR never get divorced or never meet your soulmate?

845 WYR your spirit animal was an inchworm or a dung beetle?

846 WYR dance a polka every day at noon for a week or wear only polka dot clothing for a week?

847 WYR eat the world's stinkiest cheese or down a whole jar of pickles in one sitting?

848 WYR be a member of the fashion police or the grammar police?

849 WYR know how to fix cars or how to outfox the opposition?

850 WYR have a TV in every room in your house or have a room in your house just for shoes?

851 WYR stick by the golden rule or have a golden goose?

852 WYR be able to reverse one decision every day or be able to pause time for a minute every day?

853 WYR have a blast or get a blast from the past?

854 WYR have a fear of buttons or feel compelled to push all buttons (especially big red ones)?

855 WYR bite your tongue every time you chew something or get a paper cut every time you touch paper?

856 WYR be the life and soul of the party but secretly feel depressed or have people think you're boring while you're really content with life?

857 WYR have your ducks in a row or duck and dive?

858 WYR be a driving instructor or a diving instructor?

859 WYR be addicted to eating dirt or eating soap?

860 WYR have a fear of water or be addicted to eating ice?

861 WYR always use the rule of thumb or have a green thumb?

862 WYR make it law that children should be seen and not heard or people over the age of seventy-five shouldn't drive?

863 WYR be under someone's thumb or stand out like a sore thumb?

864 WYR play by the rules or bend the rules?

865 WYR not know how to cook or not know how to drive?

866 WYR lose all your teeth or all your hair?

867 WYR be only able to whisper or only able to shout?

868 WYR never gain weight or never get sick?

869 WYR prepare a Thanksgiving meal for twelve people or give a speech in front of 112 people?

870 WYR own thirty pairs of socks or thirty hats?

871 WYR find your dream job or true love?

872 WYR be ten years older than your sibling or ten years younger?

873 WYR be someone's rock or rock the boat?

874 WYR be a stand-up comedian or a one-man band?

875 WYR never own a house or never own a car?

876 WYR kiss a crocodile or tickle a bear?

877 WYR be a cheesemaker or a winemaker?

878 WYR be an art freak or be a freakshow on the dance floor?

879 WYR be a city slicker or a country bumpkin?

880 WYR be the hider or the seeker in a game of hide and seek?

881 WYR walk the talk or walk the line?

882 WYR be shy or work-shy?

883 WYR read the book or watch the movie?

884 WYR never marry or never have children?

885 WYR your pet lived twice as long as normal or was twice as intelligent as normal?

886 WYR have your pride hurt or have to swallow your pride?

887 WYR be sitting on a gold mine or be worth your weight in gold?

888 WYR be weird and wacky or shrewd and sagacious?

889 WYR stop doing something you do daily or start doing something new on top of what you do daily?

890 WYR have to run to save your life or eat food out of a trash can to survive?

891 WYR daydream about things you've done or things you'd like to do?

892 WYR clean rest stop toilets or a slaughterhouse for a living?

893 WYR visit the land of the rising sun or the land of milk and honey?

894 WYR be able to grow at will or be able to shrink at will?

895 WYR hear the sound of silence or the sound of children playing?

896 WYR have no eyebrows or no eyelashes?

897 WYR have a job that pays $100 an hour but lets you work from home or a job that pays $180 an hour but requires you to be physically present?

898 WYR be as good as gold or be born with a silver spoon in your mouth?

899 WYR have the odds stacked against you or be the odd one out?

900 WYR get lost in the pages of a book for four hours or lose four hours on Facebook?

901 WYR never steal a robe from a hotel or never steal a kiss from someone who is in a relationship?

902 WYR save someone from drowning or save a goal in soccer so your team wins?

903 WYR be stranded in a desert with just a pocketknife or stranded in a jungle with only a rope?

904 WYR be trapped in an underwater cave with only thirty seconds of air or three hours of air and no hope of rescue?

905 WYR be the only person in town who doesn't have a car or the only person in town who does have a car?

906 WYR count your steps out loud as you walk or count backwards from ten before going through any door?

907 WYR be able to travel through time or through dimensions?

908 WYR be frugal or stubborn?

909 WYR follow a will-o'-the-wisp or stay on the beaten path?

910 WYR your hair never tangled or your feet never got cheesy?

911 WYR work twelve-hour shifts for three days each week or work offshore for three weeks and have three weeks off?

912 WYR see imaginary spiders or feel imaginary spiders?

913 WYR scream out loud in a movie theater or ugly cry in a movie theater?

914 WYR your parents never cried happy tears or your children never cried sad tears?

915 WYR never fire a gun or never be mugged?

916 WYR create a punishment for people who take all the red Skittles or people who leave an empty toilet roll holder?

917 WYR have a huge imagination or a photographic memory?

918 WYR have a full body wax or wax five cars by hand?

919 WYR push over someone's snowman or step on someone's sandcastle?

920 WYR have 330 people at your family reunion or thirty-three?

921 WYR sleepwalk or sleep talk?

922 WYR be named after a color or a virtue?

923 WYR earn someone's respect or earn someone's gratitude?

924 WYR end all illegal animal trading or have your favorite animal become extinct?

925 WYR binge-watch TV all day or binge on junk food all day?

926 WYR have a strong opinion or sit on the fence?

927 WYR knock over the first domino in someone's long line or knock down someone's house of cards?

928 WYR not be able to use a corkscrew or a can opener?

929 WYR never have another bad thought or never get invited to another good party?

930 WYR be considered "gifted" or "special"?

931 WYR be hypercritical or a hypocrite?

932 WYR be half-human, half-fly or a reverse mermaid (merman)?

933 WYR be someone to rely on or be reliably unreliable?

934 WYR never bite off more than you can chew or never bite the hand that feeds?

935 WYR not be able to open any closed doors or not be able to close any open doors?

936 WYR compromise on where you live or where you go on vacation?

937 WYR be an expert calligrapher or an expert bingo caller?

938 WYR hold a grudge or hold the record for "the most sticky notes on the face in one minute"?

939 WYR be someone who gets the ball rolling or someone who can roll with the punches?

940 WYR be impressive or be an impressionist?

941 WYR have your face slammed into a cake or have a door slammed in your face?

942   WYR put your finger into a yawning dog's mouth or kiss a duck?

943   WYR ride on the roof of a car or ride in a supermarket shopping cart?

944   WYR eat food in a supermarket before paying for it or crash a wedding party?

945   WYR pee outdoors or pee in the sink?

946   WYR dress up as a robber with a stocking on your head or as a bandit with a dish towel as a poncho?

947   WYR eat a brilliant meal in a bad restaurant or an awful meal in an amazing restaurant?

948   WYR get your tongue pierced or be a nude life model in an art class?

949   WYR have a partner who snores in bed or talks in their sleep?

950   WYR be a fast talker or a slow eater?

951   WYR let it go or fight tooth and nail to hold on to it?

952 WYR know the true meaning of freedom or the true meaning of peace?

953 WYR give up your most prized possession or give up a $100,000 prize?

954 WYR never doubt yourself or never do anything spontaneous?

955 WYR enjoy simple pleasures or strive to experience the finer things in life?

956 WYR never tell a white lie or never see red?

957 WYR have someone to watch over you or watch the world go by with friends?

958 WYR hit the dance floor or hit the hay?

959 WYR be able to talk your way out of trouble or be a guest on a talk show?

960 WYR be someone who can't hit the broad side of a barn or someone who is prone to hitting the roof?

961 WYR have an attic full of things to remind you of your past or just one photograph?

962   WYR grow old gracefully or be the oldest swinger in town?

963   WYR fall on hard times or fall from grace?

964   WYR lie about your likes and dislikes on a date or lie about your experience in a job interview?

965   WYR never be depressed or never have to eat humble pie?

966   WYR play hardball or play hard to get?

967   WYR only be able to eat cold food for the rest of your life or only be able to take cold showers?

968   WYR have sand in your underpants or honey in your footwear?

969   WYR have everything you drop be gone forever or be unable to say goodbye to workmates every day without crying?

970   WYR have your eyes stay closed for five seconds whenever you blink or your mouth stay open for five minutes when you yawn?

971   WYR burst into tears or burst into song whenever you're hungry?

972   WYR hear a buzzer every time something touches your lips or make a beeping sound when you chew?

973   WYR be trapped in a room full of spiders or one filled with snakes?

974   WYR be unable to make any facial expressions or start drooling whenever you see someone you like?

975   WYR babies cry when you look at them or dogs howl when you go near them?

976   WYR go upstairs on your hands and knees or go downstairs on your butt?

977   WYR chug everything you drink or have your mouth stay open all day?

978   WYR create a punishment for people who jump lines or people who shout into their phones?

979   WYR wake up with an upside-down face or with your arms and legs attached backwards?

980   WYR go to work on a hippity-hop or by jumping in a sack?

981   WYR get an electric shock every time you receive a text message or every time you touch someone?

982 WYR spend a day with everything in life moving in slow motion or a day when you do everything twice as fast?

983 WYR get a one-off one minute of free shopping in a store of your choice or a personal assistant for a week?

984 WYR feel compelled to yell "Shark!" whenever you swim in the sea or "Stick 'em up!" whenever you go into a bank?

985 WYR lose your internet connection whenever you open the fridge door or have the fuses blow every time you sneeze?

986 WYR develop an irrational fear of trash cans or be afraid of your own shadow?

987 WYR have the music stop whenever you get up to dance or have a fly go in your mouth every time you yawn?

988 WYR carry a rose between your teeth or burp loudly whenever you speak?

989 WYR sound like a hyena when you laugh or sound like a donkey when you cry?

990 WYR wake up every morning with a new $100 bill in your pocket but not know where it came from or wake up every morning with a new $50 bill in your pocket and know where it came from?

991 WYR everyone always laughed at your jokes or you received at least one compliment every day?

992 WYR be able to take pictures by blinking your eyes or memorize words by running your finger over them?

993 WYR not be able to use (speak or write) the letter "w" or have everything you say repeated back to you?

994 WYR have a small snail living in your ear or a small worm living in your nose?

995 WYR not shower for a week or not brush your teeth for a week?

996 WYR take one step back after every two steps forward or clap your hands in time with every step you take?

997 WYR narrate everything you do or carry your partner on your back?

998 WYR grow a tail or an extra leg?

999 WYR be able to teleport or own a clone of yourself?

1000 WYR marry for love or money?

About Us

We're an odd bunch of fun, quirky, and creative authors who love writing thought-provoking questions. And we're on a mission to spark engaging discussions.

We've all experienced awkward silence situations and resorted to superficial chitchat and small talk to pass time.

The authors here at *Questions About Me* are on a mission to end dull conversations. We created the *Questions About Me* series to invigorate conversations and help you get to know people better – including yourself.

Put down your phone, switch off the TV, and use our *Questions About Me* books to unlock endless conversational possibilities, provide an abundance of fun memories, and develop deeper relationships.

www.questionsaboutme.com

Also by Questions About Me

3000 Unique Questions About Me

2000 Unique Questions About Me

1000 Unique Questions About Me

Made in the USA
Monee, IL
02 April 2023

31023898R10060